Trudie Hart
Illustrated by Stuart Trotter

Hippo Books
Scholastic Publications Limited

Scholastic Publications Ltd.,
10 Earlham Street, London WC2H 9RX, UK

Scholastic Inc.,
730 Broadway, New York, NY 10003, USA

Scholastic Tab Publications Ltd.,
123 Newkirk Road, Richmond Hill,
Ontario L4C 3G5, Canada

Ashton Scholastic Pty. Ltd.,
P O Box 579, Gosford, New South Wales,
Australia

Ashton Scholastic Ltd.,
165 Marua Road, Panmure, Auckland 6,
New Zealand

First published by Scholastic Publications Limited, 1989
Text copyright © Mary Douglas, 1989
Illustrations copyright © Stuart Trotter, 1989

ISBN 0 590 76074 2

All rights reserved
Made and printed by Cox & Wyman Ltd, Reading, Berks
Typeset in Plantin by AKM Associates (UK) Ltd.,
Southall, London

CONTENTS

Introduction

You don't have to be a true romantic to enjoy this book, but it helps! *Stupid Cupid* is packed full of fun, and all of it on the subject of love and romance.

There are hundreds of romantic jokes . . .

> What are hot, greasy and very romantic?
> *Chips that pass in the night.*

And not-so-romantic jokes . . .

> ROBIN: You remind me of the ocean; all wild and romantic.
> *SALLY: You remind me of the ocean too.*
> ROBIN: Do I really?
> *SALLY: Yes, you make me sick.*

We've got silly rhymes . . .

> The rain makes everything beautiful,
> It makes the flowers blue.
> If the rain makes everything beautiful
> Why doesn't it rain on you?

And lots of amazing facts . . .

> According to American experts, men and women looking for a partner should buy themselves a dog. Apparently, people are eight times as likely to stop

1

for a chat with you in the street if you have a dog than if you're on your own.

And as well as all that, you can do our quiz and discover whether you really *are* romantic, read dozens of crazy love stories, learn how to send secret love messages using fans and flowers, find out all you'll every need to know about St Valentine and discover how to tell whether you'll be lucky in love by reading your palm. And that's not all!

So come on, don't be bashful and shy. Just turn the page and start a new romance!

Crazy Couples

Here we go with a hundred crazy jokes about the sillier sides of love and romance!

Adam and Eve were having a row in the Garden of Eden. "I've had enough," said Eve. "I'm leaving!"
   "Where are you going?" asked Adam. "You don't have a mother to go home to!"

ROBIN: Did you hear that the cow and the camel have just had a baby?
THEO: What is it?
ROBIN: A milkshake with huge lumps.

Have you heard about the two boa constrictors who got married last week?
They had a crush on each other.

Why did Henry VIII have so many wives?
Because he liked to chop and change.

It was Valentine's Day morning and Theo rang up his girlfriend Cleo. "Happy Valentine's Day," he said. "Will you marry me?"

"Yes," said Cleo. "Who is that speaking?"

PATSY: *I love Danny, he reminds me of my favourite boxer.*
EMMA: Frank Bruno?
PATSY: *No, Rover.*

Who were the world's smallest star-crossed lovers?
Gnomeo and Juliet.

ROBIN: My girlfriend has a very nice personality.
DANNY: *My girlfriend's not very pretty either.*

Two logs were sitting together in the fireplace. "I'm burning with love for you," said the boy log.

"Don't make such a fuel of yourself," said the girl log.

THEO: And this is a picture of my girlfriend sitting on a donkey.
CLEO: *Very nice. Tell me, which one is the donkey?*

Two women were having a cup of tea and a chat. "My husband's an angel," said one.

"I'm sorry to hear that," said the other. *"Mine's still alive."*

ROBIN: You remind me of the ocean, all wild and romantic.
SALLY: *You remind me of the ocean too.*
ROBIN: Do I really?
SALLY: *Yes, you make me sick.*

Did the sparrow fall in love with the blackbird at first sight?
No, but he egged her on.

Why did the biscuit cry?
Because her boyfriend was a wafer a week.

TIM: *My girlfriend's gone on a tropical fruit diet. She eats nothing but bananas and coconuts.*
TOM: Has she lost weight?
TIM: *No, but she's great at climbing trees.*

A couple were looking round a beautiful old stately home. "Excuse me, sir," said an attendant, "but your wife has just fallen down the wishing well in the garden."

"*It works!*"

DANNY: My girlfriend's not bad looking. She's got nice, even teeth.
THEO: *It's just a pity about the odd ones.*

What kind of flowers can kiss?
Tulips!

EMMA: *My boyfriend took me to that new disco last night.*
DANNY: Did you enjoy it?
EMMA: *No, it made me cry.*
DANNY: Why?
EMMA: *We couldn't get in!*

Theo and Patsy went to the cinema to see *Nightmare on Elm Street*. "Oooh," said Patsy, "it's so scary! I've got this horrible, cold slithery feeling down my spine!"

"*Aha!*" said Theo. "*I was wondering where my ice-cream went.*"

CLEO: *I've got this new boyfriend. He's called Dad.*
TOM: That's an usual name.
CLEO: *He was named after his father.*

Where do Eskimo boys and girls go to meet each other?
A snowball.

TOM: Did you hear that Sally's getting engaged to an X-ray specialist?
TIM: *Wonder what he sees in her?*

A couple were smooching at the disco. "Darling," said the girl, "I'm so happy. I could go on dancing like this forever."
    "You mean you don't ever want to be able to dance any better?"

PATSY: Boys keep saying I'm beautiful.
EMMA: *What vivid imaginations they have!*

What did Lady Hamilton say to Lord Nelson?
"You're the one-eye love."

Have you heard about the short-sighted tortoise who fell in love with a crash helmet?

DANNY: Will you love me even if my hair goes thin?
SALLY: Of course I will. Who wants fat hair anyway?

CLEO: I wish I had a penny for every boy who's asked me to go out with him.
EMMA: What would you spend it on? A packet of chewing gum?

What did Cinderella say when the chemist lost her photos?
"One day my prints will come."

ROBIN: Will you be my wife one day?
PATSY: I won't be your wife for a single minute!

Two little girls were sitting on the wall of the churchyard watching a wedding. First everyone arrived and went into the church for the ceremony, then they all came out and had their photographs taken. One little girl was puzzled. "Why did the bride change her mind?" she asked her friend.

  "What do you mean?"

  "Well, she went into the church on the arm of one man, and now she's holding hands with another!"

8

THEO: *I haven't slept for days.*
SALLY: Is it because you love me?
THEO: *No, it's because I sleep at night!*

Why did the elephant tie a knot in his trunk?
So that he wouldn't forget Valentine's Day.

ROBIN: Last night I dreamt that I went out with the most beautiful girl in the world.
PATSY: *What was I wearing?*

What's the difference between a happily married man and one who's been rejected?
One kisses his missus and the other misses his kisses.

CLEO: Why won't you buy me a fur coat? I'm sure Adam bought Eve a mink!
DANNY: *No, they both wore bearskins.*

What did the boy spider say to the girl spider?
"You've got a nice pair of legs, a nice pair of legs, a nice pair of legs . . ."

EMMA: My new boyfriend's a magician. He's going to saw me in two.
TOM: Is he an only child?
EMMA: No, he's got lots of half-brothers and sisters.

What happened when the two American stoats got married?
They became the United Stoats of America.

TIM: I call my new girlfriend Plum.
TOM: Because she's sweet and gorgeous?
TIM: No, because she's got a heart of stone.

What did the porcupine say when he backed into a cactus?
"Is that you, darling?"

PATSY: You're late! I've been waiting for you for hours.
DANNY: I hurt my foot.
PATSY: That's a lame excuse.

A young couple had been married for only a few weeks when Aunt Flossie came to stay. She was a very bad tempered, demanding old lady and, worst of all, she showed no sign of wanting to go home. One day the husband came home from work to find his wife crying in the kitchen. "What's wrong?" he asked.

"It's your Aunt Flossie. I can't put up with her for a day longer," sobbed his wife. "She does nothing but moan and complain."

"*My* Aunt Flossie?" said the husband. "I've only been putting up with her because I thought she was *your* aunt!"

What are hot, greasy and very romantic?
Chips that pass in the night.

EMMA: *I'm never going out with Leo again!*
PATSY: But I thought it was love at first sight?
EMMA: *I took a second look!*

What was the name of the engineer's wife?
Bridget.

Good advice: remember that is better to have loved a short person than never to have loved a tall.

SALLY: Stop acting like a fool!
THEO: *But I'm not acting!*

CLEO: *I used to go out with a well-dressed musician.*
DANNY: What did he wear?
CLEO: *Cords.*

A very shy couple had been going out with each other for more than 20 years, but the man was too nervous to ask his girlfriend to marry him. Eventually, on her 40th birthday, she plucked up the courage to say, "Don't you think it's about time we were married, Albert?"

"Yes, I do," said Albert. "The problem is, at our age who'd have us?"

EMMA: *Tim asked me yesterday if I liked his company.*
ROBIN: And do you?
EMMA: *I don't even know what company he works for!*

What happened when the two lice got married and moved to a new house?
They gave a louse-warming party.

What did the Egyptian mummy say to his girlfriend?
"Em-balmy about you."

How did the Eskimo know that his girlfriend had chucked him?
She gave him the cold shoulder.

TOM: Sally's so clever! She's got brains enough for two.
ROBIN: She sounds just the girl for you!

A spotty young man was talking to his friend. "It's surprising how many girls don't want to get married these days," he said, gloomily.

"How do you know that?" asked the friend.

"Well, none of the ones that I've asked have wanted to . . ."

Sam's parents were getting a bit fed up with having him living at home with them. "Look, my lad," said his father, "you're 35 years old. It's time you found yourself a wife and a home of your own. When I was your age I'd been married for ten years."

"Yes, but you were married to Mum," said Sam. "It's different for me, I've got to marry a stranger!"

CLEO: *My boyfriend has a photographic memory.*
TIM: That sounds interesting.
CLEO: *Not really, nothing ever seems to develop.*

13

EMMA: Do you love me?
ROBIN: Of course I do. I'd die for you.
EMMA: You always say that but you never do it.

Darling, I love you but I'm worried you're going to forget me.
I'll never forget you.
Not even in a year?
No.
Not even in two years?
No.
Knock knock.
Who's there?
See, you've already forgotten me!

TOM: Why do you call your girlfriend Tonsilitis?
THEO: Because she's a pain in the neck.

A man was driving down the road with his wife in the back seat. They'd gone a few miles when a police car stopped him. "Did you know that your wife fell out of the back of the car just now?" asked the policeman.

"No," said the man, "I just thought I'd gone deaf."

SALLY: I wish my boyfriend was tall, dark and handsome.
CLEO: *If he was, he wouldn't be going out with you.*

Did you hear the story about the man who was taken to the police station and questioned by one of the officers. "Now, sir, you say that your first three wives died after eating poisonous mushrooms. And your fourth wife has just died after falling down the stairs. Doesn't it sound rather strange?"

"Not really, Officer. She wouldn't eat the mushrooms."

TIM: *Would you be angry with me for something I didn't do?*
SALLY: No, of course not.
TIM: *Well, I didn't send you a Valentine card.*

Have you heard about the man whose wife was so bossy that she wouldn't let him talk in his sleep?

PATSY: My boyfriend is a printer.
TOM: *Yes, he looks the right type.*

Did you hear about the two romantic blood cells.
They loved in vein.

EMMA: I have a hunch.
ROBIN: *No you don't, darling, you're just a bit round shouldered.*

PATSY: Robin's been telling everyone that he's going to marry the most beautiful woman in the world.
SALLY: *You poor thing – after all the time you've been engaged!*

15

PATSY: I'm going out with a cowboy!
TOM: Is he fun?
PATSY: Yes, he's always horsing around.

A young couple were sitting on a park bench. "Will you marry me?" asked the man.

"I'd love to," said the girl, "but you've had six wives already and all of them died just a week after the wedding."

"Oh, darling," said the man, "you mustn't start listening to these old wives' tales."

PATSY: My boyfriend calls me Wonder Woman.
CLEO: That's probably because he wonders whether you're a woman or not!

What happened when the monk and the nun got married?
They had to change their habits.

EMMA: Theo says I'm pretty as a picture.
DANNY: Yes you are – it's just that the frame's in a bit of a state.

What did the electrician's wife say when he came home at midnight?
Wire you insulate?

POLICEMAN: Tell me, Miss Smith, why did you punch your boyfriend on the nose?
SALLY: Because he told me my tights were all wrinkled.
POLICEMAN: That's no reason to punch him.
SALLY: I wasn't wearing tights at the time.

PATSY: I'm fed up with men. I think I'll go out with a cabbage instead.
TOM: Why?
PATSY: At least a cabbage has a heart!

Why did the nurse marry the road cleaner?
Because he swept her off her feet.

CLEO: Did you know that the most beautiful woman in the world is going deaf?
THEO: Who is she?
CLEO: Pardon?

Cleo came home one evening and went stomping up the stairs to her room. "What's wrong?" asked her mother.

"Theo forgot Valentine's Day," she said. "He's broken my heart and destroyed my whole life. And, worse than that, he's ruined my evening."

HOUSEWIFE: My husband is so romantic! He gave me flowers last week.
NEIGHBOUR: What sort were they?
HOUSEWIFE: I don't know, I haven't planted the seeds yet.

How do hedgehogs kiss?
Very carefully.

SALLY: I've proposed marriage to five different men without avail.
TIM: Try wearing a veil next time!

What's the best name for a solicitor's wife?
Sue.

How do couples dance in Arabia?
Sheik to sheik.

CLEO: Did you know that the most beautiful woman in the world is going deaf?
THEO: Who is she?
CLEO: Pardon?

DANNY: Did you hear about the two bishops in bed?
One of them even had a nightie on!
EMMA: Which one?
DANNY: Mrs Bishop!

Did you hear about the two rabbits who got married?
They went on bunnymoon to Spain.

THEO: I'm not myself tonight.
CLEO: No, I noticed the improvement.

Late one night, a spacecraft landed in the centre of town and two strange-looking space creatures got out. The first thing they saw was a traffic light glowing in the night. "I love you, earthling. Please marry me!" said one space creature.

"Oh no you don't," said the other. "She winked at me first!"

Did Adam and Eve have a date?
No, but they had an apple.

Did you hear about the lovesick hedgehog?
He fell in love with a scrubbing brush!

PATSY: I wouldn't say my boyfriend's got a big mouth, but . . .
ROBIN: But what?
PATSY: He can eat a banana sideways!

SHEEP: My boyfriend is so polite.
GOAT: How do you know?
SHEEP: Every time we go through a gate he says "After ewe."

Two men were having a drink in a pub. "It's my 20th wedding anniversary today," said one.

"Congratulations!" said the other. "Fancy being married for 20 years."

"Oh, no," said the first man, "not 20 years – I've 20 wives!"

DANNY: Let's get engaged!
EMMA: Are you going to give me a ring?
DANNY: All right, what's your number?

TOM: My girlfriend is so stupid she thinks the Pope lives in a vacuum.
PATSY: That's nothing. My boyfriend is so stupid he thinks optimists are people who test your eyes!

EMMA: I used to go out with a dentist.
TOM: Why did you split up?
EMMA: He got on my nerves.

SWALK

What, you may be asking, does 'SWALK' mean –
and what does it have to do with love and romance?
The answer is quite simple. 'Swalk' means 'Sealed
With A Loving Kiss', and it's one of a number of
codes that people have traditionally printed on the
back of their love letters after they've sealed them.
Here are just a few of the other codes that have been
most popular.

ITALY – I Trust and Love You
SWANK – Sealed With A Nice Kiss
HOLLAND – Hope Our Love Lasts And Never
  Dies
BOLTOP – Better on Lips Than On Paper

Next time you send a love letter, why not add one of
these messages on the back of the envelope? Or, even
better, you could make up some new codes of your
own. How about making up some suitably romantic
phrases to go with these words? And if you can't
think of anything romantic, see if you can come up
with something silly! There are suggestions for both
on page 23.

NAFF   SILLY   MOLE   LIFE

Here are some suggestions for the words on page 22.

NAFF – Now And Forever Faithful
Nigel Ate Fried Frogs

SILLY – Sweetheart, I Longingly Love You
Spies In Leningrad Ladle Yoghurt

MOLE – May Our Love Endure
Mad Opticians Lay Eggs

LIFE – Love Is For Ever
Largest Igloo For Elephants

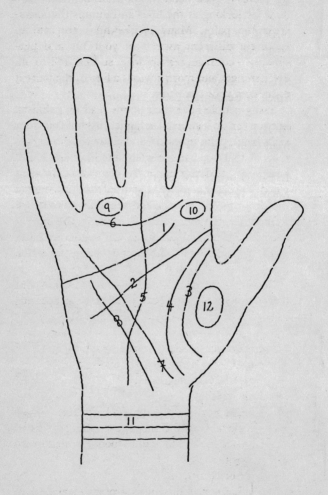

The art of reading people's characters and futures in the palms of their hands is known as palmistry. It's done by looking at the lines and bumps that criss-cross the palm. Many of the lines are said to represent different aspects of your life and personality – courage, reason, love, success and so on. The stronger and more obvious a line is, the more it influences your character.

Many people have their palms read by palmists, but you can do it yourself at home. Just hold out your right hand, palm upwards, and allow your fingers to relax so that you can see where the lines are. Don't hold your hand absolutely flat or most of the lines will disappear. Once you've spotted the lines, refer to the diagram on page 24 and see what they mean. Remember, the more obvious a line is, the more it will influence character. When you've got the knack, you'll be able to read your friends' palms for them, too.

Remember though, whatever you discover in your palm, there's not much evidence that it's an accurate reflection of your true personality and life.

1 Line of the Heart: love and devotion
2 Line of the Head: thought and reason
3 Line of Mars: aggression
4 Line of Life
5 Line of Fortune: wealth and happiness
6 Girdle of Venus: if this line is strong it's a bad sign – it shows that you're too interested in the opposite sex!
7 Line of Health
8 Via Lascivia: if this line is strong it means you're unfaithful and cunning in love.
9 Mount of Apollo: riches and artistic talent

10 Mount of Jupiter: ambition and pride
11 The Bracelets of Life: each of these lines is supposed to represent 30 years.
12 Mount of Venus: love and passion

Verse – and Worse!

Mary had a parrot,
She killed it in a rage –
For when her boyfriend came around
The parrot told her age.

'Twas in a restaurant they met,
Romeo and Juliet.
He had no cash to pay the debt,
So Romeo'd what Juliet.

Here I sit in the moonlight,
Abandoned by boyfriends and men,
Muttering over and over,
"I'll never eat garlic again."

Oh, how we danced
On the night we were wed.
We danced and we danced
'Cos the room had no bed!

Susan Walker is your name,
Single is your station.
Happy will be the nice young man
Who makes the alteration.

Rose are red, violets are blue,
Sugar is sweet and so are you.
And so is he who sends you this –
And when we meet I hope we'll kiss.

I love you, dear,
I love you mighty.
I wish your pyjamas
Were next to my nightie.
Now don't get flustered,
Don't go red!
I mean on the clothesline
And not in bed!

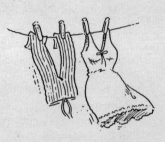

"Your teeth are like the stars," he said,
And pressed her hand so white.
He spoke the truth, for like the stars,
Her teeth came out at night.

Two in a hammock
Attempted to kiss,
When all of a sudden
They landed like sıɥʇ !

The rain makes everything beautiful,
It makes the flowers blue.
If the rain makes everything beautiful
Why doesn't it rain on you?

The bottle of perfume that Willie sent
Was highly displeasing to Millicent.
   Her thanks were so cold,
   They quarrelled, I'm told,
Through that silly scent Willie sent Millicent.

If all the boys
Lived over the sea
What a good swimmer
Susie would be.

I love you, I love you
Please be my Valentine.
And give me some bubble gum –
You're sitting on mine.

When accepting a young man called Hugh,
His girlfriend said, "Yes, I'll be true.
   But you must understand,
   Now you've asked for my hand,
That the rest of me goes with it too!"

A man and his lady love, Win,
Skated out where the ice was quite thin.
They quarrelled no doubt
And I hear they fell out;
What a blessing they didn't fall in!

The Tale of Two Piggies
Two piggy friends to market went,
Their names were Paul and Patience.
They both were sold and both were sent
To different destinations.

As the sad pair were dragged apart,
Paul said, in loving tones,
"Don't cry, we'll meet again, dear heart,
I feel it in my bones."

And meet they did, true to their wish;
Paul had not been mistaken.
He was the sausage on the dish
And Patience was the bacon.

Shall I compare thee to summer's day?
Cold, wet and miserable . . .

I know a girl called Passion.
I asked her for a date.
I took her out to dinner –
And gosh! How Passionate!

"Oh, how I miss my husband so!"
The woman cried.
And so just one more shot
At him she tried.

Here comes the bride
Sixty inches wide.
See how she wobbles up the church's aisle!
Here comes the groom,
Biting his nails in gloom,
He's looking as thin,
As a dressmaker's pin
And never again will he smile.

Will the Real St Valentine Please Stand Up?

As every true romantic knows, St Valentine is the patron saint of lovers. But who was he, and how did he become such an important saint in our calendars? The terrible truth is that no one really knows!

What we do know is that way back in the times of the ancient Romans, there was a big festival held each February 14. Boys going to the festival had to take part in a draw to find the name of the girl who was to be their partner – a bit like pulling a prize out of a lucky dip. As you probably know, the Roman Empire covered most of Europe, including Britain, and this festival became a regular time of celebration throughout the continent.

Then came Jesus Christ and the birth of Christianity. The Roman Empire crumbled, but the old Roman festival was still celebrated; after all, everyone liked to have a good time! Everyone, that is, except the early Christian priests who, according to one theory, didn't approve of all this larking around. They didn't like the idea of boys and girls dancing together but they knew they couldn't stamp it out – so they decided to change the customs surrounding the festival. Instead of boys drawing lots for the name of the girl they would go with to the festival, the priests substituted saints' names. It doesn't sound nearly as much fun, does it? One of the saints whose name appeared in the draw was St Valentine and, gradually, over hundreds and hundreds of years, the day took on his name and became St Valentine's Day. That's one theory, at least.

Another is that the old Roman festival was replaced by the custom of drawing a girl's name by lot and then sending her a gift. Over the years, so it's said, the gift was replaced by a letter and, in Victorian times, by a card.

But who was St Valentine? No one's really sure but, during the third century, a servant called Valentinus got into trouble for helping Christians who were being persecuted by the Romans. He was put in prison for this and eventually sentenced to a nasty fate. (If you're a bit squeamish you had better skip the next sentence). First he was to be beaten with sticks, then stoned and, finally, his head was to be cut off. I did warn you it was nasty! Because of the fact that he died for the Christian faith he was later made a saint and became St Valentine.

Quite how he came to be associated with love is a bit of a mystery. A legend tells that while waiting in prison for his execution Valentinus fell in love with the jailor's blind daughter and cured her sight. It's also said that on the night before his death, which is on record as happening on February 14, he wrote her a letter and signed it "From Your Valentine", but no one knows if this is really true.

To make things even more complicated there are, in fact, at least two St Valentines. As well as the one whose feast day we still celebrate there was St Valentine of Genoa, who was actually more of a romantic character. He died on May 3 – and if you think about it, it makes more sense to have a festival devoted to love and romance in May rather than in February, when everyone's still wrapped up in their winter woollies.

One professor, Henry Kelly, who has been studying the subject for years, says that all the blame lies at the door of Queen Isobel of Bavaria. Back in the Middle Ages she turned her court into the Court of Love and knights and ladies gathered there to discuss romance – and to fall in love too. This idea caught on, and soon other Courts of Love were established around Europe. Isobel launched her Court of Love on "the day of my Lord St Valentine", probably meaning St Valentine of Genoa. Unfortunately, she got him and his date muddled up with the other St Valentine and, according to Professor Kelly, we've all been celebrating the error ever since!

As if all that wasn't enough, there seem to be rather a lot of hoax St Valentines around. You may have visited Roman Catholic churches and cathedrals and seen "relics" of saints' bodies. It was a common practice to keep the bodies and bones of dead saints so that their followers could come and visit the remains. Well, there are bits of so-called St Valentines all over Europe. In Spain there are two bodies said to be his, and a head. In Rome there's another body and other bits. And elsewhere there are a number of other relics of St Valentine. Confusing, isn't it?

And now for the final confusion: some experts refuse to believe that St Valentine's Day is anything to do with St Valentine at all! They say that the word "valentine" is derived from an old French word "galantine", which means "a ladies' man". We also get the word "gallant" from the same French source.

So there you have it – or don't have it! No one knows for sure which theory, if any of them, is correct. Perhaps *you* have a better explanation of why St Valentine is the patron saint of lovers, or why we celebrate love and romance on February 14?

Romantic Reads

Have you read any of these crazy romantic books?

Is This Love? by Midas Wellbe
Our First Year Together by Annie Versary

Jilted! by Anne Gwish
Let's Go Out by Tamara Knight
How to Tell When You're in Love by U.B. Shaw
My Wedding Day by Trudy Light
Over the Threshold by Carrie Mee
I Married a Millionairess by Ivor Fortune
The Bridegroom was Late by Willie Makit
Lover's Knot by Izzie Tied
The Boyfriend's Return by Gladys Back
A Lovers' Quarrel by Thayer Thorry
Love Comes Tomorrow by Claire Voyant
Make Your Own Bouquet by Rose Bunches
The Wedding Service by Neil Down
How to Propose by Percy Vere
The Fastest Wedding Ever Known by Marion Haste

Say it With Fans

These days, the idea of going to the disco or on a date with your mother in tow seems ridiculous, but in the eighteenth and nineteenth centuries young ladies were chaperoned everywhere by their mothers or a servant to ensure that they didn't speak to any strange men. You can imagine how frustrating this was for the girls, who were desperate to talk to handsome young chaps, so they cleverly devised a secret language which enabled them to flirt right under the noses of their mothers.

In those days most women carried fans, so the young ladies (and some older, married ladies too!) communicated messages to their true loves by holding the fans in different ways. The only problem with this system was that some ladies didn't understand the fan language. The would stand in the ballroom, innocently fanning themselves and sending all sorts of strange messages!

What good is this information to you? Well, although you'd look pretty stupid waving a fan around, it should be possible to copy some of the movements using, for example, an exercise book in class, or a pencil, or even just tapping your cheek or ear with your finger. This kind of language could be very useful in a noisy disco where it's impossible to talk. But it's most useful of all when you want to keep your relationship a secret from others.

Here are just a few examples of the original fan language. Why not try them out and find new and different ways of using the signals? Once you've perfected your own secret language you can teach your boy or girlfriend too. They can tell you how much they love you in the middle of a geography lesson – and no one will ever know!

I love you – Open the fan and hold it up to your face, hiding your eyes, or, with the fan closed, point quickly to your heart.

I don't love you – Hold the fan open and pointing downwards, with the back of your hand on top. Make a movement as if you're shooing someone away.

I am interested in you – Hold the open fan up to your chin, then slowly lower it and extend your hand to the other person, almost as if you are offering the fan to them.

We're being watched; we mustn't talk – Fan your face gently and then bring the fan up and hold it above your head for a few moments.

Don't let anyone know our secret – With the fan closed, gently touch your left ear.

Yes – With the fan closed, touch your right cheek.

No – With the fan closed, touch your left cheek.

Get lost – Hold the closed fan up to your mouth and yawn.

In Ireland one stag party ended with the bridegroom being rowed out to the middle of a lake and marooned there by his two friends. He couldn't swim, so they threw the oars overboard and then jumped into the water and swam to the bank. They planned to come back and collect him in time for the ceremony the next morning, but both of them had such bad headaches from their hangovers that they forgot. It was only when they arrived at the church for the ceremony and the groom wasn't there that they realized what was wrong!

And another groom who nearly missed the wedding was found on board a train travelling from Stafford to London by British Rail staff. His friends had bundled him into a large Post Office mail bag and loaded him into the guards' van. Hearing strange noises coming from the sack, the guard rescued him. He had just enough time to catch a train back to Stafford for the wedding!

Something similar happened to Frank and Sue-Lynn Clarke who had met through their favourite hobby, hot air ballooning. They had decided that rather than drive off from the wedding reception in a boring old car, they would fly away in a balloon. Frank organized it all and he and his new bride climbed into the basket and waved goodbye to their friends. Up went the balloon, on course for a field several miles away where they planned to land. Then, without warning, the wind changed and the balloon went hurtling towards a clump of trees, tangling the basket in the branches. Sue-Lynn escaped unhurt but poor Frank broke both arms and spent his honeymoon in plaster.

The Silliest Love Stories Ever Told

Just in case you're in danger of taking love and romance too seriously, here's a collection of some of the most unusual love stories ever told. A few of them are genuinely romantic and touching, but the rest are hilariously funny, because the strangest things seem to happen when people fall for each other! But of course, before you fall in love you need someone to fall in love with – and that's where we start . . .

Before you can fall in love and get married, you have to meet each other – and that was a problem for Lynette Barber of Basingstoke, who couldn't seem to

find the right man. She advertised in Lonely Hearts columns for two years and, during that time, went on 200 dates, but without any luck. One of the men who replied to her advert described himself as "mature". When 25-year-old Lynette met him, she discovered that he was 72 years old! Eventually, deciding that there was no Mr Right for her, Lynette gave up the search. Soon after that she fell in love with the man who had been living next door all the time!

But for most people it's once you've met your partner that the problems really begin! When Gavin Stuart decided to propose to his girlfriend Caitlin, he took her out for a meal to the best restaurant he could find. He also arranged a rather special surprise. For their dessert, Gavin asked the chef to make a lovely heart-shaped gateau and to hide the diamond engagement ring he'd bought inside one half. All went according to plan and Caitlin was thrilled when the cake arrived. The waiter cut her half and Gavin, waiting to see the look on her face when her spoon hit the engagement ring, took a mouthful of his own gateau and bit into it – and broke one of his back teeth. Instead of spending a romantic evening with his fiancée, as he had planned, Gavin had to be taken to the dentist for emergency repair work.

Most people meet their partners and marry within a few years, but there are some couples who like to take things at a more relaxed pace. Take, for example, Elizabeth Allen and Joe Fonge from Oxfordshire, who went on their first date in 1917. Fifty years later they decided that they knew each other well enough to get married – and so in 1967 they did! Fifty years may seem a long time, but it's not the record. Octavio Guillen and Adriana Martines, from Mexico, took even longer to reach the altar. They met as youngsters and in 1902 they became engaged. Neither of them wanted to race into marriage, however, so they waited a few years – 67 years, to be precise. Eventually in 1969, when they were both 82 years old, Adriana and Octavio decided that the time was right and walked down the aisle together.

Let's hope that their marriage got off to a better start than this one reported in the last century.

> "MARRIED: Moses Alexander, aged 93, to Mrs Frances Tomkins, aged 105, in Bata, New York, on June 11, 1831. They were both taken out of bed dead the following morning."

Other people don't take so long and like to get things over and done with quickly. Take the case of one young couple in America, who had what was possibly the fastest marriage ceremony ever. Having decided on the spur of the moment to get married, they raced off to the local courthouse where Judge Charles Galbreath was presiding. (In America judges can marry people.) They asked him if it would be possible to keep the ceremony short and he agreed. "Do you want to get married?" he asked.

"Yes," they said.

"You are," he replied. And they were!

There was a special wedding held in Jeddah, Saudi Arabia in 1978, when a proud Arab father gave away two of his daughters to be married at the same ceremony. As the two heavily-veiled brides and the two grooms exchanged their vows, the registrar mixed up their names and married the wrong girl to the wrong man. The poor father decided that the only way for things to be put right was for both girls to divorce and marry again, but a few days later his daughters announced that, far from being upset, they were quite happy with their husbands.

In 1972, Mr Darsun Yilmaz, who lived at Damali on the Black Sea, fell in love with his neighbour's daughter. She, however, was not interested in him.

Mr Yilmaz was not put off by this and, late one night, he arrived in the neighbour's garden carrying a ladder which he placed beneath the girl's window. He climbed up to her room, wrapped her in a blanket and carried her back down to his car.

After driving a few miles he stopped to unwrap his beloved. As he pulled back the blanket he discovered he had made a terrible mistake, for there in the moonlight he saw not the girl of his dreams but her ninety-year-old grandmother! Even worse, Granny was very angry and she beat him up!

Most wedding ceremonies go without a hitch, but one held at Hastings in 1986 takes the prize for the most disastrous. First of all the vicar went down with appendicitis on the morning of the wedding and had to be rushed to hospital. A young replacement vicar was called at the last moment to conduct the ceremony. Then the bride arrived at the church to find that the groom was not yet there. He had got locked in the bathroom at his home and had to climb out of the window. On the way down the drainpipe he'd ripped his trousers. When he finally arrived at the church the bride was in tears, thinking he'd jilted her. During the ceremony the emergency vicar was very nervous and got the couples' names wrong; he had to start all over again.

When, finally, it was over and the guests went outside to have their pictures taken, the bride's father slipped on the wet grass and cracked his head against a gravestone. This was too much for the bride, who fainted and was taken to hospital in the same ambulance as her father. The groom and his new mother-in-law followed the ambulance in his shiny new car – until a bus ran into the back of them.

"Everyone said it would be a day to remember for the rest of our lives," said the bride later, "but personally I'd prefer to forget it."

Judy and Patrick Crane got to church on time and the ceremony had just started when a panicky pigeon, having flown in but being unable to find its way out, started to dive-bomb the congregation. The service was halted while attempts were made to coax it outside, but nothing worked. The apologetic vicar sent bride, groom and their guests to the vicarage to have a cup of coffee while he went to find a farmer with a gun. It didn't take long and soon the poor pigeon had been disposed of. When the little bridesmaids heard what had happened they were very upset and cried throughout the service.

When Keith Watkins and Caroline Fullerton were married in Leicester, they had problems with the old iron gratings in the floor of the church. Karen, dressed in a long white wedding gown, walked down the aisle and caught her heel in one of these grids. Her shoe was firmly stuck and no one could move it, so she took the other one off too and continued down the aisle in her bare feet. The ceremony went well until it was time for the best man to hand Keith the ring. He was nervous and dropped it – straight down a grating. The wedding had to stop while the vicar, the guests and the members of the choir lifted up the grid and searched for the lost ring!

Listeners to Radio Four recently heard the tale of Steven Hale and Julie Bradshaw's wedding. Things began to go wrong even before the ceremony. First of all, only 10 of the 70 guests who had been invited were able to come. Then the best man was late picking up Steven, who had to beg a lift to the church. Once the ceremony was over all the guests enjoyed a reception on board a boat that cruised up and down the Thames – but, unfortunately, the boat broke down five times and in the end burst into flames. That night Steven and Julie boarded a plane for their honeymoon in Crete, but they hadn't been in the air long when it was announced that they were going to have to make an emergency landing in Munich because one of the passengers was suffering pains in his leg. It was eventually discovered that this was because his trousers were too tight! When the newly-weds finally reached their hotel on Crete they found that their room had been double booked and, no sooner had they sorted that out, than there was a terrible hurricane. And even when they got home there was one more disaster still in store for them. The man who had taken the photos at their wedding revealed that not a single picture had come out; they didn't even have a reminder of their terrible day!

Busy Brian Delisle-Tarr didn't drop the ring; he just didn't have time to buy one for his wedding. When he parked his car outside the register office he removed a ring-shaped jubilee clip from the engine and decided that that would have to do instead. All went well and, at the appropriate moment in the ceremony, he slipped it on to his bride's finger. There was just one problem – she couldn't remove it and, after the ceremony, the newly-weds had to go round to the local fire station to have it cut off. (The ring – not the finger!)

If you have ever been a bridesmaid or a pageboy you will know that it can be a rather boring job. Six-year-old Tiffany Wells thought so when she was the bridesmaid at her big sister Cheryl's wedding. When her sister went up to the altar she gave Tiffany her bouquet to hold. No one was paying Tiffany much attention and she whiled away the ceremony by picking all the petals and leaves off the flowers. When Cheryl came back down the aisle and reached out for her bouquet, all she had left was a bunch of stalks.

Eight-year-old Stevie Hyde from Hertford was even naughtier. His brother Nicholas got married in April 1986 and, after the wedding reception, the bride and groom set off in their car for a night at the posh Savoy Hotel in London before flying off on honeymoon. When they arrived and opened the car boot they found that Stevie had stowed away with the luggage. It was too late for someone to come and collect him and he couldn't go home on his own, so he spent the night at the Savoy with the newly-weds!

The night before they get married many men have a stag night out with their male friends, and this can sometimes lead to disaster. One young doctor who had had too much to drink the night before, woke up on the morning of his wedding to find one leg in plaster – all the way from the ankle to the thigh. His friends told him that he had fallen down some steps and broken it, and although he couldn't remember anything that happened he believed them. He hopped through the wedding ceremony on crutches and hobbled off on honeymoon with his new wife. It was only when he got back that his "friends" revealed that he hadn't broken his leg at all. They'd just put the plaster on for a joke.

The married life of Kenneth Kiehn and his wife Donna got off to a difficult start when they posed for wedding pictures on a balcony. "Back a bit," said the photographer, and they stepped backwards – and over the edge of the balcony. When they were rescued from the fountain some 30 feet below, they were, according to Donna's mother, still holding hands.

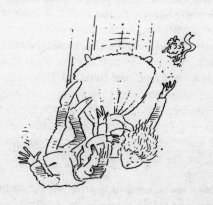

Accidents at weddings are nothing new. On 26 May 1886 *The Times* reported an accident that had occurred after a wedding service in Bethnal Green, east London. The friends and relatives of the bride and groom lined up outside the church and, as was the custom, threw rice at the happy couple. Unfortunately some of it landed in the groom's eye and he had to be taken to the local doctor, who tried to remove it. By now he was in great pain and his eye had been damaged, so instead of going off on honeymoon with his new wife he had to spend a week in hospital. Because of accidents like these, people started throwing confetti.

Of course, some people don't get as far as the church. A few years ago an attractive American lady called Blanche Blair was stopped for speeding and taken to court in Sacramento, California. She had a perfectly clean record except for 24 speeding offences in the last few months. Why, asked the judge, had she suddenly started to break the law? "Because I've fallen in love with you and there's no other way I can get to see you," said Miss Blair, and asked him for his photograph.

'No,' said the judge, and fined her $50.

In folk tales we're used to hearing of a princess's hand being offered in marriage as a prize, but it doesn't happen much in real life. However it *did* happen in 1896 when the Greeks decided to revive the ancient tradition of the Olympic Games. Naturally they wanted their own sportsmen to do well, so for the first prize of the marathon a Greek millionaire offered the winner a year's worth of free dinners and the hand of his daughter in marriage. His offer worked, and the winner of the marathon was a Greek runner. He gratefully accepted the free dinners but unlike the princess in fairy stories, he declined the girl's hand in marriage. He had to; his wife told him so!

48

At least one person has gone to a wedding not knowing that it was *he* who was going to be married. In 1985 Colin Entwhistle turned up at the registry office for what he thought was his friend's wedding. He couldn't see his girlfriend Julie anywhere, so he went inside – and when he came out he was married. Julie had decided to surprise him and had made all the arrangements without telling him what was going on. Fortunately Colin didn't seem to mind too much.

Oxford student Simon Norris was so keen to impress his girlfriend on St Valentine's Day that he arranged to cook a romantic dinner. As well as delicious food there was a red rose on the table and soft music in the background, and his room was lit with dozens of candles which cast a romantic glow over the evening. Simon's girlfriend was impressed – until the candles set light to the curtains and the whole room caught fire. They both had to be rescued by firemen who came to put out the blaze. Not a very romantic way to end the evening, you might think, but even worse was to come. A few days later his girlfriend told Simon that she didn't want to see him any more. She'd fallen in love with the young fireman who had helped her down the ladder!

There's another story told about a man who, 70 years or so ago, fell in love with a rich young lady who lived in Sussex. One weekend he went to stay at her family's very large and very old house, determined to ask her to marry him. He was given a lovely room to stay in, full of antique furniture and with a beautiful and very valuable old carpet on the floor. During the night he woke up feeling thirsty, reached for the glass of water he'd put on the bedside table, and heard something fall over. He couldn't think what it was and he was feeling very sleepy, so he just turned over and went back to sleep. The next morning he got up – and realized that he'd knocked over a bottle of ink which had spilled all over the priceless carpet. Horrified, he left the house without asking the girl to marry him.

A few months later, when he felt it was safe to return, he went to see the girl again, still determined to propose to her. When he arrived at the house he was shown to the room where the girl's mother was having tea. The young man explained that he would like to speak to her daughter and the lady went to find her. Very nervous, the young man sat down on a cushion on the sofa. Unfortunately, it wasn't a cushion after all, as he realized the moment he sat down. It was in fact the mother's Pekingese dog, and he had killed it! He ran straight out of the house and, it is said, never came back.

Poor Michael Eastwood was unlucky too. He booked up to go on holiday with a group of young single people, hoping that he would meet the girl of his dreams. Sadly it didn't work out like that. Mike was the only person to book the holiday, so he spent a fortnight in Ibiza on his own.

Another sad tale: a young Canadian man fell in love with a Scottish girl he met on holiday and wrote to her every day for more than a year, pouring out his romantic feelings. Unfortunately his plan backfired – she married the postman who delivered all the love letters!

A happier story is told about shop assistant Michael O'Connor who, in 1907, was sacked from his job and sent to jail because one sunny spring morning he had impulsively kissed a lady customer, Miss Hazel Moore. Ten years later Mr O'Connor received a letter from Miss Moore's solicitor. She had died and in her will she had left Mr O'Connor £20,000 in memory of the only time in her life when a man had kissed her.

One of the worst traffic jams ever known in Rio de Janeiro, Brazil, was caused by two teenagers who stopped their car for a red traffic light and had a quick kiss while they were waiting. The lights changed to green but they didn't stop kissing. People stuck behind them began to honk their horns but only when furious motorists tried to pull them apart that it was discovered that the dental braces they were wearing on their teeth had got tangled together. A dentist had to be called before they could be separated!

Two very romantic people were film stars Humphrey Bogart and Lauren Bacall. If you're a film fan you may have seen them together in some wonderful black and white movies. They first met on the set of a film called *To Have and Have Not*, in which Miss Bacall had the line, "If you need anything, just whistle." They fell in love during the film and were later married. When Humphrey Bogart died in 1957, his wife placed a small gold whistle in his coffin. On it was written that line from the film.

Also romantics were a young couple who appeared in court together for an offence. The judge sentenced them each to a month in detention but, before they could be taken away to separate cells, they superglued their hands together so that they couldn't be parted.

The image that most of us have of Queen Victoria is definitely an unromantic one but, in fact, she and her husband Prince Albert had a wonderful love story. She had been queen for three years and he was just a German prince when they met and almost immediately fell wildly in love. Victoria had to propose to him because, as she wrote in her diary: "Albert could not propose to the Queen of England. He would never have presumed to take such a liberty!" When he died just 20 years later she was heartbroken and, for the rest of her long life, she had his rooms kept exactly as they had been when he was alive and clean clothes laid out for him each day.

Another romantic couple from the past were Elizabeth Barrett Browning and her husband, the poet Robert Browning. In her teens, Elizabeth had an accident that hurt her back and, for the next 25 years, although there was nothing much wrong with her, she lived the life of an invalid and very rarely went out. In 1840 she started writing to the handsome young poet Robert Browning and, in 1846, they decided to get married. However, Elizabeth's father was very jealous and refused to allow her to marry – so they eloped together and had a secret wedding, after which they went to Italy and lived very happily there for the rest of Elizabeth's life. Their story became a romantic legend and Elizabeth wrote many poems about their love. This is one of them from her collection entitled *Sonnets from the Portuguese*. It's one of the greatest love poems ever written.

"How do I love thee? Let me count the ways.
I love thee to the depth and breadth and height
My soul can reach, when feeling out of sight
For the ends of Being and ideal Grace.
I love thee to the level of every day's
Most quiet need, by sun and candlelight.
I love thee freely, as men strive for Right;
I love thee purely, as they turn from Praise.
I love thee with the passion put to use
In my old griefs, and with my childhood's faith.
I love thee with a love I seemed to lose
With my lost saints' – I love thee with the breath,
Smiles, tears, of all my life! – and, if God choose,
I shall but love thee better after death."

Equally romantic was the poet Dante Gabriel Rossetti. When his wife died he was heartbroken and, as a gesture of his love, he buried the book containing all his poems in her coffin. Seven years later, however, he began to regret doing his – so late one night the coffin was dug up and the poems removed and disinfected. They were later published and made Rossetti famous.

Sometimes love makes people behave in a very eccentric way. Richard "Beau" Nash was very famous in his time as the leader of the social scene in Bath, and friend of the future king. When he died in 1761 his girlfriend was so distressed that she vowed she would never sleep in a bed again. For the next 17 years she lived in a huge, hollowed-out tree near Bishopstrow in Wiltshire and, true to her word, never again slept in a bed.

Many people still think of actress Marilyn Monroe as one of the most beautiful women the world has ever known, and most actors longed to star in a film opposite her. But when actor Tony Curtis got the chance in the film *Some Like It Hot* he was not impressed by her looks. In the film he had to shoot a number of scenes dressed as a woman, wearing high heels and a skirt and heavy make-up – which he found very uncomfortable. Miss Monroe kept him waiting for hours, which made him understandably furious. When filming finished everyone wanted to know what it had been like to kiss the most beautiful woman in Hollywood. They were in for a surprise. The unromantic Mr Curtis told them, "I'd rather kiss Hitler than Marilyn Monroe."

Young people like to think that they are the only ones who can be romantic but this story about Evaristo Bertone, an 85-year-old Sicilian man, proves otherwise. One day he came across a love letter written to his wife Adriana. He was so mad with jealously that he attacked poor Adriana, who was also in her 80s and stabbed her in the shoulder. Adriana was surprised; she couldn't remember getting a love letter from another man. Evaristo showed it to her, she read it – and then she pointed out that he had written it himself more than 50 years before. "He's so romantic," said his wife, "and his eyesight is so bad that I had to forgive him."

Valentine cards can be almost as dangerous as love letters when it comes to getting you into trouble. Colin Rust, a student from Manchester, was furious when his girlfriend Hayley showed him three Valentine cards that she'd received from boys at school. The boys had signed their names and written a loving message. Colin caught up with each of the three boys in turn and challenged them to a fight. During one fight he broke the other boy's nose and the police were called in. Colin soon found himself in court to explain why he'd been fighting. Strangely enough, all three of the boys protested that they hadn't sent cards to Hayley. Everyone was puzzled – until Hayley herself owned up. She admitted that she'd sent the Valentine cards to herself, and forged the messages and signatures, to see if Colin really loved her!

When a lady called Vera Czermak discovered that her husband had been going out with another woman she decided to end it all by jumping out of the window of their third-storey flat. She came round later in hospital, still alive. Her fall had been broken by a man walking beneath the window. The man was her husband, Mr Czermak, and he'd been killed when his wife landed on him.

Other romantic gestures can backfire too. In September 1986 Chris Stokely from Esher planned a secret surprise for his girlfriend Jan by planting 400 crocus bulbs on her lawn while she was away. Sadly, after Christmas Chris fell in love with another girl and he and Jan didn't see any more of each other. Then came the spring, and up through Jan's lawn popped 400 purple crocuses spelling out, in letters two feet tall, CHRIS LOVES JAN FOR EVER.

And finally, the romantic story to top them all. In 1986 Rose and Antony Johnson held a "Not a Wedding" party to celebrate the fact that their divorce had come through. All the guests who had attended their original wedding and reception were there, and everyone had a great time – including Rose and Antony. By the end of the evening they'd decided that the divorce was a mistake and couldn't wait to get married all over again!

Quiz: Test Your Romance Rating

Are you one of the world's greatest romantics or do you think romance is a waste of time? Do you charm the opposite sex or do they run away laughing when you come near? You can find out how you rate in the romantic stakes by answering the questions in this quiz. The first five questions are for everyone; after that there are separate sections for boys and girls.

1 Have you ever sent anyone a Valentine card?
  a) Only as a joke.
  b) No.
  c) Yes.

2 Where would you choose to go for a Valentine's Day night out?
  a) The local Wimpy Bar.
  b) A football match.
  c) A beautiful moonlit beach on a warm night.

3 Imagine that you are choosing some romantic music for Valentine's Day. Which of these bands or singers would you choose?
  a) Michael Jackson and Prince.
  b) Motorhead and Def Leppard.
  c) Rick Astley and Lionel Richie.

4 Have you ever written a love poem for someone?
  a) Yes, and thrown it away.
  b) Not on your life!
  c) Yes, and sent it to them.

5   On a Valentine's Day date, which film would you
    choose to see?
    a) *Crocodile Dundee.*
    b) *Rambo.*
    c) *Romancing the Stone.*

Boys

If you're a boy, answer the questions in this section.

B6 Imagine you're choosing a bunch of flowers for
    a girl you're going out with on Valentine's Day.
    What would you buy?
    a) A bunch of carnations.
    b) A cactus.
    c) A single perfect rose.

B7 What kind of meal would you like to take your girlfriend out for on Valentine's Day?
  a) Steak and kidney pudding and apple pie and cream.
  b) Hamburger, fries and shake.
  c) Fillet steak and strawberries.

B8 If you could fly anywhere in the world for St Valentine's Day, where would you choose to go?
  a) London or Paris.
  b) Benidorm or Scunthorpe.
  c) The Taj Mahal or the Pyramids.

B9 Have you ever complimented a girl on what she is wearing or how she looks?
  a) Once or twice, if I think she's looking especially fantastic.
  b) Never – she might think I'm getting keen on her!
  c) Often – I always think the girls I go out with are beautiful.

B10 You've been out for a wonderful Valentine's Day date. Now you've brought your girlfriend home and you're standing on the doorstep. Imagine gazing into her eyes. What would you say?
  a) Can we go out again tomorrow night?
  b) Did you know that your make-up is smudged?
  c) Thank you for the best evening of my life . . .

Girls

This section is for girls to answer.

G6 Which of these books would you prefer to read?
   a) *Adventures on a Pony.*
   b) *Grow Your Own Vegetables.*
   c) *Endless Love.*

G7 Which of these things would you give your boyfriend for Valentine's Day?
   a) A bottle of aftershave.
   b) A pair of orange and purple spotty socks.
   c) A red satin heart-shaped cushion you'd made yourself.

G8 What would you wear for a romantic Valentine's Day picnic in a field by a river?
   a) Jeans and a T-shirt.
   b) Wellington boots and a plastic mac.
   c) A pretty dress.

G9 Which of these TV characters or personalities
    would you rather be?
    a) Michelle from *EastEnders*.
    b) Dame Edna Everidge.
    c) Paula Yates.

G10 Imagine that your Valentine's Day date has
    just arrived to take you out. He gives you a
    single red rose. What is your reaction?
    a) I wish he'd given me a whole bunch of
        them.
    b) What a ridiculous thing to do!
    c) This is going to be the perfect romantic
        evening.

Now you've answered the questions, add up how
many As, Bs and Cs you have scored and turn to page
121 to find out whether you're a great romantic or a
Valentine's Day flop.

Flowery Language

"Lingua flora", or "the language of flowers" is an almost forgotten art these days. It all started with the ancient Greeks who used to send messages to their true loves in the form of bouquets of flowers. Each type of flower had a different meaning and, by choosing the right mixture, Greek men could send their girlfriends quite complicated messages.

The language of flowers became tremendously popular in Victorian times and whole books were written on the subject. Perhaps it was easier for shy Victorian men and women to say it with flowers than say it themselves! These days not many people understand the language any more – so don't read too much into the fact that the man next door gave your mum a bunch of carnations for her birthday – but it could be fun to send secret flower messages to your girl or boyfriend. And you could also send messages to other people. How about a sunflower for your bossiest teacher?

Here's a list of the most commonly available flowers and their meanings:

anemone – anticipation
buttercup – wealth and riches
camellia – excellence

candytuft – "I don't care"
carnation – true love
clover – happiness
cyclamen – "I don't care about you"
daffodil – "I'm sorry"
dahlia – instablity or unreliability
daisy – innocence
forget-me-not – "Don't forget me"
foxglove – insincerity
French marigold – jealousy
fuchsia – taste and elegance
geranium – comfort
harebell – grief
hawthorn – hope
holly – living happily together ever after
hollyhock – ambition
honeysuckle – faithfulness
hyacinth – sorrow
ivy – married love
jasmine – friendship and happiness
lavender – "I acknowledge your love"
lilac – the first dawn of love
lily – purity
lily of the valley – the return of happiness after
    trouble
lupin – dejection
mimosa – sensitivity
pansy – "I'm thinking tenderly of you"
pinks – perfection
roses: red – true love
          yellow – jealousy
          white – "I am worthy of your love"
          dark red – shame
snowdrop – consolation
sunflower – haughtiness

sweet pea – delicacy
tulip – "You have beautiful eyes"
violet – faithfulness

Love At First Fright

It's not just people who fall in love – monsters do too! And to prove it, here's a selection of monster romantic jokes.

MANDY MONSTER: My boyfriend's so romantic. He gave me flowers yesterday.
GRETA GHOST: Roses?
MANDY MONSTER: No, triffids!

"*Doctor, doctor can a man fall in love with a giant hairy monster?*"
"Of course not, it's impossible!"
"*Then do you know anyone who'd like to buy a very large engagement ring?*"

MALCOM MONSTER: That girl rolled her eyes at me.
DADDY MONSTER: Well roll them straight back, she might need them later.

Does Count Dracula believe in love at first sight?
No, but he does believe in love at first bite!

MARVIN MONSTER: *My girlfriend swallowed a pencil last night.*
GORDON GHOUL: Is she all right?
MARVIN MONSTER: *Yes, this morning she sat down and wrote me this love letter.*

Why do demons always marry ghouls?
Because demons are a ghoul's best friend.

MRS MONSTER: I went to Frankenstein's wedding last week. His bride has a pretty face.
MR MONSTER: *Only if you can read between the lines.*

Once upon a time there was a sad and lonely monster who couldn't find a wife, so he advertised in his local newspaper. A lady monster wrote back and, for several weeks, they sent letters to each other. Eventually they decided it was time to meet. "I'd better tell you this before we meet, so that you don't get too much of a shock when you see me," he wrote to her. "I'm bright green, 10 feet tall, covered in spots and I have two heads, three eyes and three arms. I'll meet you at the monster disco on Tuesday at eight o'clock, unless you feel that I'm too ugly for you."

"Looks mean nothing to me," wrote back the lady monster, "so long as you have a kind heart. P.S. Would you wear a pink carnation on Tuesday evening so that I can recognize you?"

DOCTOR: But why did you marry a ghost?
MAN: *I don't know what possessed me!*

Count Dracula has announced that, contrary to rumours, he is not going to marry Viscountess Vampira; they are just good fiends.

MRS GHOUL: Don't you ever get lonely?
DR FRANKENSTEIN: No, I can always make myself a new girlfriend.

What did Mrs Ghost cook for Mr Ghost for their wedding anniversary dinner?
Ghoulash.

Where do royal monsters get married?
In Westmonster Abbey.

MRS GHOUL: My husband wants an electrical gadget for his anniversary present.
MRS SPOOK: How about an electric chair?

What happened when the pink monster saw the ghost?
It was love at first fright.

MUMMY MONSTER: Why aren't you going out with your boyfriend?
MANDY MONSTER: I've chucked him. I discovered he had a glass eye.
MUMMY MONSTER: How do you know that?
MANDY MONSTER: It came out in conversation.

What tunes do ghosts smooch to at the disco?
Haunting melodies.

MALCOLM MONSTER: Darling, let me take you to the Blood Ball.
SKELETON: Sorry, my heart's not in it.

GRETA GHOST: My boyfriend tells me he loves me, but I don't believe him.
GORDON GHOST: Why?
GRETA GHOST: I can see right through him.

What did the skeleton say to his girlfriend?
"I love every bone in your body."

69

MANDY MONSTER: I used to go out with a vampire.
GRETA GHOST: *Oh, vampires! They're just a pain in the neck.*

What aftershave do boy monsters wear for a date?
Brute.

MALCOLM MONSTER: I'm in love with a girl who has green hair all down her back.
GORDON GHOST: *What a pity it's not on her head.*

Did you hear about the girl monster who wasn't pretty and wasn't ugly?
She was just pretty ugly.

MANDY MONSTER: *Look, my boyfriend's just given me an engagement ring!*
MUMMY MONSTER: What kind of stone is that in the middle?
MANDY MONSTER: *A tombstone!*

What did the invisible man say to his invisible girlfriend?
"It's wonderful not to see you again."

70

SPOOK: I've given my monster boyfriend the push.
GHOUL: But why? He was kind, clean, polite and friendly . . .
SPOOK: Exactly – a total failure.

MARVIN MONSTER: My girlfriend's just lost 20 pounds of excess fat in less than a minute.
GORDON GHOUL: That was some diet!
MARVIN MONSTER: She didn't diet – I just chopped her head off.

Ten Things You (Probably) Didn't Know About Valentine Cards

The earliest Valentine on record was written in 1415 by the French prince Charles, Duke of Orleans, when he was locked up in the Tower of London. It can still be seen in the British Museum.

Until the 1800s everyone made their own Valentine cards and wrote their personal love poems inside. One of the most popular types of Valentine was a cut-out, like a paper doily, with patterns of hearts and flowers and doves. You could try making your own at home. All you need is some white paper, a pencil and a pair of scissors. Fold the paper in half and then in half again, draw a pattern of hearts and flowers on one side and then cut out the bits of paper that you don't need.

In the 1800s when people began to buy their cards rather than make them themselves, they had a beautiful selection to choose from. Many were hand made from silk, with embroidered pictures and messages; others were made of layers of lace and embossed paper. These are now valuable and many people collect them. Why not see if your grandparents, or even *their* grandparents, kept any of the Valentines they received? You could make your own Victorian Valentine card by painting a pretty pattern on a piece of card and adding some lace from paper doilies and a pretty picture taken from a magazine. Decorate it with any bits of ribbon you can find and paint flowers in the corners. It's much more romantic than a modern Valentine card!

The Victorians were very fond of pop-up Valentines. When you opened them, Cupid or a bunch of flowers popped out. There were even some rude pop-up Valentine cards; in one of them, which showed a lady on the front, you pulled a tab and her dress popped up, leaving her with nothing on!

In Britain one very popular type of Valentine card took the form of a cheque or bank note made out to the Bank of True Love. Some of these cards looked so much like the real thing that they were banned and people who had bought them were told to send them back to the manufacturers. Apparently some people were actually using them as real money!

Can you think of anything less romantic than a picture of a tomato on a Valentine card? And yet during the 1800s lots of cards were decorated with tomatoes. The reason was that, in those days, the tomato was known as the Love Apple – and so it was the perfect thing to have on a Valentine.

Many old Valentines came complete with a small envelope stuck to the card, in which suitors placed a tiny lock of their hair.

The Victorians printed Braille Valentine cards for blind people.

Those romantic Victorians who wanted to write their own poem in their Valentine cards but couldn't think what to say, could buy a special book called *The Ladies and Gentlemen's Sentimental Valentine Writer*. It showed how to write rhymes and suggested ideas for winning their true loves' hearts.

Not all Valentines were slushy and romantic. During the 1800s comic and rude cards were popular. One showed a picture of a not-very-attractive girl and beneath it the rhyme:

"Sweet maiden with the love-sick eyes,
And face as pale as the moon:
The man who wins you for a prize
Need never buy a wooden spoon."

In Victorian days you could buy a rude Valentine to tell someone you didn't want to marry them, or that you thought they were too old, or that they talked or drank too much. Maybe it's a custom we should adopt these days. Can you think of anyone to whom you wouldn't mind sending a rude Valentine card?

Stupid Cupid

You may have been wondering about the cheeky little chap with the bow and arrow who features in the title of this book. Where does Cupid come from? And why is he always pictured as a naked boy with bow and arrows? The truth is that his origins go back thousands of years – as far as ancient Greek mythology, in fact. In those days he was called Eros and he was the Greek god of love. He was usually pictured as a beautiful winged boy and, in those days, he was quite a serious character, more concerned with establishing peace and love than romances. If you ever go to Piccadilly Circus you can see the famous statue of Eros there.

Then the Romans, whose gods were based on the Greek ones, took over Eros, christened him Cupid and jazzed up his image. Instead of being a serious character, Cupid became a bad lad who shot arrows of desire at people, making them instantly feel romantic. In the Middle Ages the word "cupidity" was added to the English language. Someone who suffers from cupidity wants to grab all the wealth and possessions he can – and he also wants to grab as many ladies as possible! So Cupid was no longer a nice character. He was a hard-hearted trouble-maker, creating chaos whenever he fired his arrows. Often his idea of a joke led to unhappiness and tragedy, and people actually feared that he might disrupt their lives by making them fall in love with someone totally unsuitable.

Over the hundreds of years since then people have begun to understand the world in different ways and belief in gods like Cupid has waned. As people began to worry about him less, his image began to change.

If you ever have the chance to go to a famous art gallery which has a good collection of old paintings, you may well see how he was portrayed by artists from the sixteenth century onwards as a plump, mischievous little angel with a quiver full of arrows and his bow at the ready. He ceased to be a dangerous character and became merely a naughty little scamp.

It was during the Victorian era that the final changes to Cupid became obvious. He is shown on many of their Valentine cards looking like a little winged child – very sweet and innocent, and bearing absolutely no resemblance to the original god. The

Victorians also dressed him up in a variety of outfits, including a skirt and a long shirt, because they didn't like to see him naked. Fortunately since then there has been a backlash against this sweet image and once more we're seeing Cupid as a naughty little mischief-maker, and this is the way he appears on the cover of this book. As you can see, he's wearing a nappy; it's cheating, we know, but we really couldn't have his bare bottom on the back cover – could we?!

Great Mistaikes!

These errors have all appeared in local papers and reports around the country. Have a look in your local paper and see if you can spot any yourself!

"Last week we announced the wedding of Miss Teresa Clark and Mr Glenn Kirkpatrick. This was a mistake."

"Come to the Red Lion for your wedding reception in our beautiful dining-room – seats 30-50 people. Or for the smaller celebration, have a party in the comfort of our open log fire."

"MARRIAGES. HILTON-SPIVEY. On July 9th, 1986, in bath, Ray and Kitty."

"Miss Rachel Ferris and Mr Brian Gibson were married at the United Reformed Chuch, Winchester on Saturday. Bridesmaids were Miss Emma Knightley and Miss Michelle Gibson. The best was Mr Tim Phipps."

"HONEYMOON COTTAGE IN ROMANTIC BRONTE COUNTRY. Seventeeth century luxury cottage, perfect for honeymooners. Sleeps 5."

"The bride, who was given away by her father, wore a punk dress and a dark blue bridegrooom's two young nieces . . ."

"WEDDING DRESS FOR SALE. Beautiful white lace wedding dress, size 12. Worn twice. Bride no further use. £50."

"The bride carried a bouquet of yellow roses and fuschias to match the bridegroom."

"The engagement of Miss Frances Oliver and Mr William Headley was announced on Friday. The couple met when Miss Oliver ran over Mr Headley in her car."

"Miss J. Seeley and Mr P. Rathcool, both aged 26, went to school together in Chertsey. Their wedding on Saturday will bring their twelve-year romance to an end."

Knutty Knockers

You never know when love's going to come knocking
at your door . . .

Knock, knock.
Who's there?
Mischa.
Mischa who?
Mischa so much while you've been away!

Knock, knock.
Who's there?
Ivor.
Ivor who?
Ivor a big bunch of roses for you.

Knock, knock.
Who's there?
Ken.
Ken who?
Ken I kiss you?

Knock, knock.
Who's there?
Fozzie.
Fozzie who?
Fozzie hundredth time, will you marry me?

Knock, knock.
Who's there?
Pyjamas.
Pyjamas who?
Pyjamas round me, honey, hold me tight.

Knock, knock.
Who's there?
Ivan
Ivan who?
Ivan engagement ring for you!

Knock, knock.
Who's there?
Alec.
Alec who?
Alec you very much.

Knock, knock.
Who's there?
Iris.
Iris who?
Iris you'd marry me!

Knock, knock.
Who's there?
Ida.
Ida who?
Ida like to go out with you.

Knock, knock.
Who's there?
Jemima.
Jemima who?
Jemima coming to the disco with me tonight?

Knock, knock.
Who's there?
Jester.
Jester who?
Jester called to say I love you.

Knock, knock.
Who's there?
Jill.
Jill who?
Jilted at the altar!

Knock, knock.
Who's there?
Mary.
Mary who?
Mary me.

Knock, knock.
Who's there?
Ewan.
Ewan who?
No, just you an' me together for ever!

Knock, knock.
Who's there?
Wooden shoe.
Wooden shoe who?
Wooden shoe like to marry me?

She Loves Me – He Loves Me Not

When you had your meal last night, were two forks crossed at your place at the table? If so, according to tradition, it means that you're going to have a romance very soon. Do the joints of your fingers crack when you pull them? If they do, you're due to go out with a new boy or girlfriend. Next time you drop a spoon, don't blame yourself for being clumsy. Folklore has it that people drop spoons when their true love thinks of them.

There are hundreds of different customs associated with falling in love and predicting who you will marry. Whether any of them is actually true it's impossible to say – but it might be fun to try a few of them out and see what happens!

Who Will Be Your Sweetheart?

Perhaps the best-known way of predicting who you will marry involves peeling an apple in one long,

continuous strip without the skin breaking. Then throw it over your right shoulder. It is supposed to fall to the ground showing the initial of your sweetheart. Some people say that this method works best on Midsummer's Day or May Day or even on Hallowe'en, and others recommend that you say this rhyme before you throw the peel over your shoulder:

"I pare this pippin round and round
Upon the ground to flounder.
My love to me it will reveal –
Let's hope he's not a bounder!"

And remember to pick the peel up once you've tried this custom!

If you don't like apples, try onions. Take an onion, peel it, wrap it in a clean hanky and put it under your pillow. You should dream of your beloved. The only drawback to this one is that raw onions in bed make the sheets and pillowcases pretty smelly!

Or try this. At midnight on New Year's Eve, girls are said to be able to take a look at the man they'll marry by sitting and brushing their hair in front of a mirror in a room lit only by a candle. If the girl is going to marry in the next year, the face of her husband is said to appear in the mirror, looking over her shoulder. Very spooky!

Tradition has it that the first boy or girl you see on the morning of Valentine's Day is destined to become your husband or wife. In the past, when people took these things more seriously than they do now, there were stories of girls who waited for hours with their eyes shut until the young man of their fancy came along. Why not try it next Valentine's Day, just for a laugh?

84

If you get up early enough on May Day morning you can race down to the garden and wash your face in the dew before it disappears. Once you've done that, though, be careful; according to folklore, the first man you see after that will be your husband, and you may not fancy the postman or the paper boy.

Finally, next time you have some stewed plums or some cherries, count the stones left when you've finished the fruit using this rhyme: "Tinker, tailor, soldier, sailor, rich man, poor man, beggarman, thief". If you have five stones you're destined to marry a rich man, but if you have eight stones you'd better watch out!

And Will My Love Be True?

Once you've found your boyfriend or girlfriend, there are some old-fashioned ways of telling whether they will be true to you. One of the most popular ones involves picking a flower and pulling off the petals one by one saying, "She loves me, she loves me not," as you do so. The final petal will tell you whether or not you're loved.

It's said that if a boy can encircle a girl's wrist with

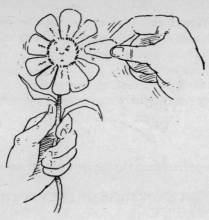

the fingers of one hand, he loves her. If he can't do it, he doesn't. And if you're still not sure whether your true love is true, take a hair from their head and stretch it between your dampened thumb and forefinger. If it comes out straight it means that they are true, and if it goes all curly it means they are going out with someone else. But before you have a huge row and break up, perhaps it would be a good idea to bear in mind whether their hair was curly to begin with!

Cupid Was Here!

Here's a collection of the funniest graffiti around!

THERE'S A SHORTAGE OF PRETTY GIRLS
AROUND HERE.
I don't care how short they are, just tell me where I
can find them!

BUY THE PENGUIN BOOK OF ROMANTIC
POETRY.
I didn't know penguins could write poetry!

MARRIAGE IS A GREAT INSTITUTION.
But I don't want to spend my life in an institution . . .

My girlfriend thinks she's a strawberry.
SHE IS IN A JAM, ISN'T SHE?

A HAPPY MARRIAGE IS A QUESTION OF
MIND OVER MATTER.
I don't mind and you don't matter!

MY TEACHER FANCIES ME. SHE KEEPS
PUTTING LITTLE KISSES ON MY HOME-
WORK.

Would you say a bachelor is an unaltared male?

A bachelor never Mrs anyone!

I'M GOING OUT WITH A MONK.
So you've got the Abbey habit.

LOVE IS BLIND.
That's why I always kiss boys in the dark.

An apple a day keeps the doctor away – but an onion
a day keeps everyone away!

I love Phil. Carol.
I love Phil. Susie.
Hard luck, Carol. Phil.

Before you meet your handsome prince you have to
kiss an awful lot of toads.

CINDERELLA MARRIED FOR MONEY!
She really put her foot in it . . .

I LOVE MY TEECHER.
Fried or boiled?

SAY IT WITH FLOWERS.
Hit her over the head with a bouquet.

It's In The Stars

Are you one of the millions of people who check your horoscope every day in a newspaper or magazine? If you do, you probably already know that as far as astrologers are concerned, our lives are written in the stars from the moment we are born. They believe that the pattern of stars and planets at the time of birth has a huge effect on our characters, the way we live our lives – and love, of course. Do you know which birth sign you are? You can look it up on this chart.

Aries	21 March to 20 April
Taurus	21 April to 21 May
Gemini	22 May to 21 June
Cancer	22 June to 23 July
Leo	24 July to 23 August
Virgo	24 August to 23 September
Libra	24 September to 23 October
Scorpio	24 October to 22 November
Sagittarius	23 November to 21 December
Capricon	22 December to 20 January
Aquarius	21 January to 19 February
Pisces	20 February to 20 March

According to astrologers, each sign of the zodiac has its own characteristics and everyone born under that sign shares them. Here is a general outline of the characteristics usually associated with each sign. Have a look and see what kind of personality you are supposed to have.

Aries – straightforward, energetic, brave and positive

Taurus – determined, patient, hard working and logical

Gemini – active, quick-witted, impatient and a bit of a show off

Cancer – sensitive, caring, old fashioned and careful

Leo – courageous, confident, arrogant, energetic and vain

Virgo – polite, clear headed, creative and critical

Libra – balanced, charming, optimistic and calm

Scorpio – busy, responsible, powerful, cruel and sexy

Sagittarius – helpful, enthusiastic, independent, reckless and cheerful

Capricorn – wise, generous, dependable but a bit lonely

Aquarius – imaginative, caring, independent and a bit selfish

Pisces – sensitive, creative, proud and sometimes unrealistic

Does it give an accurate description of your personality? Or perhaps technically you're a Libra, for example, but you feel as if you should really be a Gemini? Unfortunately it's not possible to change your zodiac sign so you're stuck with the one you're born under whether you like it or not.

As you can imagine, some of the signs get along together better than others – and, the theory goes, some people are more compatible than others because of the signs they were born under. It makes sense when you look at it. If you put a bold, bossy Leo together with an ambitious, powerful Scorpio you're just asking for a fight! And a quick-witted, fast-moving Gemini might find it very difficult to live or work with a plodding patient Taurus. So for love and happiness, astrologers believe that we should all look for someone of a compatible sign whom we will be able to get along with. Here are the partners they recommend for each sign.

Aries – Gemini, Leo, Virgo, Sagittarius
Taurus – Cancer, Capricorn, Virgo, Pisces
Gemini – Aries, Leo, Libra, Aquarius
Cancer – Taurus, Virgo, Scorpio, Pisces
Leo – Aries, Gemini, Libra, Sagittarius
Virgo – Taurus, Cancer, Scorpio, Capricorn
Libra – Gemini, Leo, Sagittarius, Aquarius
Scorpio – Cancer, Virgo, Capricorn, Pisces
Sagittarius – Aries, Leo, Libra, Aquarius
Capricorn – Taurus, Virgo, Scorpio, Pisces
Aquarius – Aries, Gemini, Libra, Sagittarius
Pisces – Taurus, Cancer, Scorpio, Capricorn

Don't worry if you find that your boyfriend or girlfriend's birth sign isn't among those listed against yours. It doesn't mean that you're not going to get on. There's no scientific proof that when it comes to love and marriage, astrology works. And you'll probably only have to look at the members of your own family to find a happy couple who, astrologically speaking, shouldn't be getting along together. But if you've been unlucky in love in the past, maybe next time you meet a boy or a girl you'd like to go out with you should start by asking them which sign of the zodiac they were born under. Who knows – love may be written in the stars!

The Facts of Love!

This collection of weird and wonderful facts about love, marriage and romance will enable you to surprise your friends with some amazing information.

WARNING: Some of these facts are a bit rude. Don't tell them when the vicar or your great-grannie come to tea!

The Chinese don't like kissing very much. In fact until Westerners arrived and brought the habit with them, the Chinese hardly ever kissed each other at all. In fact, when all is said and done, China isn't a very romantic country. There's a law preventing people from marrying until the man is 26 years old, so if couples meet and fall in love before then they have to wait a long time before they can marry.

We traditionally wear the wedding ring on the third finger of the left hand because it was believed in ancient times that there was a vein directly linking that finger to the heart.

These days we accept that Catholic priests, and in particular the Pope, do not get married. However this has not always been the case. In the past many popes have had children. Pope John XII was actually killed by a man who found him making love to his wife!

Good news for fatties: a worldwide survey of men's taste in women discovered that, worldwide, more men preferred plump women to slim ones. Bad news for fatties: in the western world more men like slim girls than fat ones.

Giraffes can't kiss, but they show affection by rubbing their necks together.

In the original romantic fairytale, Cinderella's slipper was made not of glass but of fur. The confusion happened when the story was translated into English from the French. Even so, glass slippers sound much more romantic than furry ones, don't they?

American experts say that men and women who are looking for a partner should buy themselves a dog. Apparently people are eight times more likely to stop for a chat in the street if you have a dog with you than if you're on your own.

Casanova had a reputation as the world's greatest lover, and in memory of his conquests we call a boy or man who has great charms with women a Casanova. But not many people know that Casanova spent the last 10 years of his life working as a boring old librarian.

Some men are never content with having just one wife or girlfriend. Take the example of King Solomon of Israel, who had no fewer than 700 wives and lots of girlfriends besides. Just imagine trying to remember their birthdays!

Romantic German statesman Karl Wilhelm von Humboldt wrote a 100 line poem in honour of his wife every day for 40 days.

In Victorian times people were very prudish and some people refused to place a book written by a man next to a book written by a women – unless in real life the authors were married!

Lonely American cats and dogs looking for partners can use the services of their very own marriage bureau. It could only happen in America, couldn't it!

Turkey and India aren't very romantic countries. Until recently kissing was banned from all the films shown there.

Rude Fact

King Ethelred the Unready was king of England in the tenth century. He was also, as far as we know, the only English king to be found in bed on his wedding night not only with his new wife but also his mother-in-law!

In Moslem countries it is very easy for a man to divorce his wife. All he has to say is "I divorce you" three times to her, and that's it.

In 1922 a 24-year-old English woman appeared in court and admitted to 61 bigamous marriages in a space of just five years.

What is "the anatomical juxtaposition of two orbicularis oris muscles in a state of contraction"? It's the technical description of a kiss!

If you worry because you're not very beautiful, take some comfort from the knowledge that if beauty is only skin deep, as the saying goes, in some places it is less than 0.5 mm deep.

People were not very romantic in the seventeenth century. In Boston a man who gave his wife a quick kiss in the street one Sunday was sentenced to spend two hours in the stocks for his "obscene" behaviour.

Peggy Hopkins Joyce became one of the world's richest women. She did it by marrying five millionaires.

Any Japanese dogs who want to take out their canine girlfriends in Tokyo can go for the evening to a special restaurant where all the customers are bow-wows.

The longest kiss to be seen in a film was in the 1941 movie *You're in the Army Now*. Regis Toomey and Jane Wyman kissed for three minutes and five seconds.

The film with the most kisses is said by film buffs to be *Don Juan*, in which the actor John Barrymore has 191 kisses. That works out at a rate of nearly one a minute!

Rude Fact

Most men believe that women are attracted by muscular hairy chests, but in fact women prefer men who have small bottoms. Now you know, lads.

In the seventeenth century it was the custom for women to wear their wedding rings on their thumbs.

When King Philip the Handsome of Spain died in the 1500s his wife was so upset that she refused to let the corpse be buried. It stayed in her bed and she slept by its side every night for three years. Not surprisingly the people of Spain called her Joanna the Mad.

Have you ever wondered why the word "love" is used to mean "zero" in tennis? When written down the figure zero looks like an egg – so the French called it that, and in French "egg" is "l'oeuf". When the game came to England, instead of translating "l'oeuf" back to "zero" they retained it and called it "love".

What could be more romantic than a bath in champagne? If you'd like to give your boyfriend or girlfriend such a treat you'd better start saving because to buy a bath and fill it with 270 bottles of champagne will cost you around £3000!

The Black Widow spider is the most unromantic of creatures. She always eats her "husband" after mating, and she can get through as many as 20 of them in a single day.

97

In India nine out of 10 girls are married by the age of 20.

In North Siberia, which is part of Russia, peasant women have a way of letting a man know that they want to go out with him. They throw slugs at him.

Rude Fact

Until the eighteenth century it was thought very bad to wear a nightdress in bed. Most people slept with nothing on! And until the Victorian era, neither men nor women wore any underwear. It must have been draughty in winter!

It's difficult to believe these days when nobody turns a hair at girls wearing bikinis, that just 100 years ago women were so covered up that men thought a glimpse of an ankle very sexy. In some very prudish households, even a piano's legs were thought to be too sexy – they were covered up too!

In the sixteenth century a law was passed allowing men to beat their wives, so long as they stopped doing it at 10 p.m.

Eskimos rub noses as a sign of affection, rather than kissing.

If you go to Tibet and someone sticks his tongue out at you, don't get angry. It's the Tibetan way of being friendly.

Lucrezia Borgia, famous for poisoning her enemies, had been married four times by the age of 22.

In the Hindu religion it is considered very unlucky for a man to marry for a third time. If a Hindu man wants to take a third wife he can change the bad luck by getting married to a tree. The tree then counts as his third wife, and it is burned. Then he is free to marry wife number four.

Eleanor of Aquitaine, a queen of England who died in 1204, was very seriously into romance. She set up a special court, known as the Court of Love, in which the problems of love were discussed and judgements made. It is also believed by many experts that it was Eleanor who chose St Valentine to be the patron saint of lovers and romance.

In days of old, a knight used to go into battle carrying his lady's handerkerchief tied around his lance as a favour, or carrying a flag displaying her colours. Later, in the sixteenth and seventeeth centuries, couples had miniature pictures painted of each other and used to carry them around. These days we have photographs, so it's all much simpler!

When unromantic Peter the Great, ruler of Russia, discovered that his wife had a boyfriend, he had the man's head cut off. Then he put it in a big jar of alcohol to preserve it and gave it to his wife so that she could keep it by the side of her bed. Yuck!

The Roman emperor Nero gave his wife a very romantic gift – 500 asses. You don't think it sounds very romantic? The milk that they produced was enough for her to bathe in every day so that she could keep her skin looking lovely.

In Ancient Greece, a woman's age was counted from the day she got married. It doesn't seem fair that those women who did not marry never had a birthday!

When Sir Walter Raleigh died, his wife was so upset that she had his head embalmed and then carried it in a red leather bag for the rest of her life.

The average length of engagements in Britain is 19 months.

According to an old saying, young men's thoughts turn to love in the springtime, but experts say this is not true. Apparently young men's hormones are at their most active in the autumn and winter.

One of the most mis-matched couples in the animal world are the male and female angler fish. Mrs Angler Fish is huge and can weigh almost half a ton. Mr Angler Fish is only a few millimetres long and spends his entire life attached to the tip of his wife's nose.

Mormon leader Brigham Young had 20 wives and the Mormon religion allows all its male followers to have as many wives as they please.

According to a survey in the USA the best place to meet the man or woman of your dreams is not at a disco but at the shops or in the launderette.

When his wife Eleanor died during a journey in East Anglia, Henry II had her body carried slowly back to London to be buried. At each place the coffin stopped for the night a cross was built to commemorate Henry's love for her. Waltham Cross gets its name from the cross built there, but perhaps the most famous of all was the cross built in the village of Charing, just outside London. You can see it next time you go to Charing Cross railway station!

Haj Ahmel, who ruled Algeria, had 385 wives from different parts of the world. None of them could speak the same language and so they couldn't gang up against him.

A third of people who give their house a name call it after the place they went on honeymoon.

Researchers at Warwick University have been doing research on the smells that make people feel happy and romantic. They tested perfumes and bouquets of roses, but the winning smell was – fish and chips! So now you know, girls. Forget all those expensive perfumes and just dab some salt and vinegar behind your ears!

Men in Lancashire spend more money on their fiancées engagement rings than men in East Anglia.

One in five couples have their wedding video-taped these days.

Romantic King Edward VIII loved American divorcee Mrs Simpson so much that in 1936 he abdicated the British throne so that he could marry her. He also hated the thought of her having to handle dirty old banknotes that others had used, so each morning he gave her a wad of brand new, freshly printed notes.

The study of beauty is called kalology.

Instead of kissing, the people of Samoa like to sniff each other.

In the South Pacific, girls of the Tiwi tribe are married at birth.

It costs £1936 to have a red rose delivered to your boyfriend or girlfriend every day for a year.

Male silkworms can tell when a female silkworm moth is around. They have such a sensitive sense of smell that they can detect her up to five miles away.

A survey carried out in the USA has revealed that 24 per cent of men proposed marriage to their partner while they were in a car.

Several supermarkets in New York have what they call a "singles" night when single shoppers looking for a partner can gather and do their shopping together.

In Britain the odds against a woman marrying a millionaire are 250,000 to one.

Romance is forbidden on Mount Athos in Greece, where there are a number of monasteries that not only ban women from visiting but also ban all female animals.

A 1987 survey revealed that only one per cent of men in Britain do the washing and ironing.

The habit of toasting a woman's health originated in Ancient Rome. In those days it was customary to drink a glassful of wine for every letter of the woman's name. That might have been a good custom if your girlfriend's name was Ann Cox, but Henrietta Blenkinsop's boyfriend would probably have been too drunk to finish the toast properly!

Russian women use more perfume than the women of any other country in the world.

Rude Fact

The French translation for a "French kiss" is an "English kiss".

In the state of Minnesota in the USA it is illegal to hang male and female underwear together on the same washing line.

In India many women chew a type of nut called betel. It dyes their teeth red, which Indian men think is a sign of beauty.

In Iceland women do not change their surnames when they get married. In fact there aren't very many surnames to go round and, to avoid confusion, the telephone directory lists people by their first name.

Henry VIII was the most married English king. He had had six wives altogether and in just one year, 1536, his first wife, Catherine of Aragon, died; his second wife, Anne Boleyn, was beheaded; and he married his third wife, Jane Seymour.

Traditionally Cupid has been pictured naked on Valentine cards. This was too much for the Victorians, however, and they dressed him in a skirt.

At the wedding of King Henry I of England there was a hold up when the king and the priest conducting the ceremony had a row. The king wanted to wear his crown all the way through the marriage. The priest insisted that he take it off. It's not on record which of them won the argument.

Mills and Boon sell around 20 million romantic novels in Britain each year.

The word "bride" comes from the ancient German word meaning "the one who cooks".

In Nairobi in 1984 a 100-year-old man was married to a girl of 14. The best man was a mere 86 years old.

In Kentucky, USA, it used to be illegal for a man to buy a hat without his wife in attendance to give her judgement.

It's said by experts that most people know roughly how attractive they are, on a scale from one to 10, and look for a partner with the same attractiveness rating. That's why so many couples choose partners who look similar to themselves.

One of the world's most married women was Adrienne Cuyot of Belgium, who was engaged more than 650 times and tied the knot with 53 men over a period of 23 years. That works out at more than two husbands a year!

In the Philippines they have a special way of kissing. They put their lips together and both breathe in very quickly.

An American man was granted a divorce on the grounds that his wife cooked him nothing but pea soup to eat.

In many parts of France it is believed that if an unmarried man steps on a cat's tail he will not be married within the following year.

If you have ever been put off kissing someone because they, or you, have a cold – don't worry. According to medical experts, more people catch colds by shaking hands than by kissing.

The ancient Egyptians were the first recorded civilization to exchange rings at wedding ceremonies.

The average American woman kisses 79 men before she gets married.

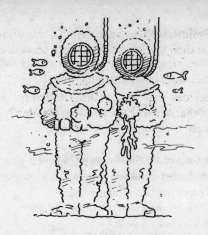

Possibly the most peculiar wedding on record occurred in 1978 when Arturo Santora and Barbara Durante were married at the bottom of the sea. Both wore deep-sea diving gear and the bride carried a bouquet made of coral and seaweed.

Rotten Romances

This chapter contains a selection of my favourite romantic, and not-so-romantic jokes!

TIM: Patsy just told me I was a dreamboat.
CLEO: More like a shipwreck, I'd say.

What's the definition of a prickly pear?
Two porcupines in love.

ROBIN: I got 20 Valentine cards last year.
DANNY: That's a lot!
ROBIN: Yes – I couldn't afford stamps to send them all!

PATSY: I've bought Tim a water-proof, rust-proof, elephant-proof watch for his birthday.
CLEO: I'm sure he'll love it.
PATSY: There's a small problem. It just caught fire.

What's pink and wrinkled and goes everywhere with Grandad?
Grandma.

What did the big telephone say to the little telephone?
"You're too young to be engaged."

THEO: I'm going out with a new girlfriend, but her feet smell and her nose runs.
TOM: Sounds to me as if she's been built upside down.

Everyone was very surprised when the old lady down the road announced that she was getting married. "But you've always said that men were stupid," said her neighbour.

"I used to," said the old lady, "but then I found one who asked me to marry him."

TIM: My girlfriend takes a milk bath every week.
SALLY: Pasteurized?
TIM: No, just up to her waist.

Have you heard the story about the boy who went to see his girlfriend's father so that he could ask for her hand in marriage? "I understand that you want to become my son-in-law," said the man.

"I don't *want* to," said the boy, "but I'd like to marry your daughter so I haven't much choice, have I?"

EMMA: My new boyfriend's very worried about catching germs when we kiss.
DANNY: So what do you do about it?
EMMA: I've found a lipstick with antibiotics in it.

A man was talking to his friend. "My wife made me a millionaire," he said.

"She must be a remarkable woman."

"She certainly is. Before we married I was a multi-millionaire."

CLEO: *I'm sick of Theo. He broke my umbrella.*
SALLY: How did he do that?
CLEO: *I hit him over the head with it.*

Tom took Patsy home to meet his parents for tea. His father shook hands with Patsy. "Is this your most charming girlfriend?" he asked.

"No," said Tom, "she's the only one I've got."

TIM: *You owe me 50 pence for that honey.*
EMMA: What honey?
TIM: *I never knew you cared!*

Why did the ant elope?
Nobody gnu.

THEO: Is that a new type of perfume you're wearing?
PATSY: Yes, it's called High Heaven.
THEO: It certainly stinks to high heaven!

What do you call two turnips who fall in love?
Swedehearts.

SALLY: I had an argument with my boyfriend last
night. He wanted to watch the football on TV and I
wanted to watch *EastEnders*.
ROBIN: Oh, which team won the football match?

"Get me Interpol, and make it quick!" said the man
to the telephone operator.

"You'll have to dial the Paris operator, sir."

"All right," said the man, and he dialled again.

"Paris operator here. How can I help you?

"I have to speak to someone at Interpol urgently."

"Do you have the number, sir?"

"No, I don't. Please hurry, it's important."

"I'm sorry, sir," said the Paris operator, "but I'll
have to put you through to Directory Enquiries.
Please hold on."

"I'm holding on," said the man.

"Hello, this is Directory Enquiries in Paris."

"Can you give me the number of Interpol – it's urgent," begged the man.

"Let me see, monsieur – the number is Paris 101010."

"At last!" said the man, and he quickly dialled the number.

"Hello?" answered a voice.

"Is that Interpol?"

"Oui."

"Thank goodness. I've forgotten my girlfriend's birthday and I want you to send round a dozen red roses this afternoon . . ."

PATSY: *Did you hear that the sheep and the rainstorm have just had a baby?*
THEO: How sweet! What is it?
PATSY: *A wet blanket.*

CLEO: I'd never marry you – not even if you were the last man in the world.
TOM: *You wouldn't get a chance – you'd be trampled in the rush.*

Patsy and Tim were out for the evening. *"Je*

114

t'adore," whispered Tim in Patsy's ear.

"Go and shut it yourself," said Patsy.

CLEO: Sally says she could marry any man she pleased.
DANNY: The problem is, she hasn't pleased anyone yet!

What did the Princess say to her knight in shining armour?
"Don't just stand there, slay something!"

PATSY: How could I ever leave you, darling?
TIM: By 'plane, or bus, or car, or boat, or train . . .

Did you hear about the elephant who just got engaged to the hippopotamus?
They're planning a big wedding.

EMMA: Will you still love me when I'm old and ugly?
ROBIN: Well I love you now, don't I?

What has a mouth but never kisses?
A river.

Sally and Cleo were in the newsagent's shop, looking for Valentine cards. "This one's got nice words inside it," said Sally. "To the only boy I've ever loved."

"Great," said Cleo. "I'll buy six of them."

PATSY: *Tom is the most amazing person.*
CLEO: Is that your honest opinion?
PATSY: *No, it's his.*

What did the snake charmer and the undertaker receive for their wedding present?
Matching "Hiss" and "Hearse" pillow cases.

DANNY: What happened to that stupid blonde girl that Theo used to go around with?
CLEO: *I dyed my hair . . .*

What name is given to a woman who gets married for money?
Marigold.

"What's wrong?" asked Patsy when she found Emma crying in the school playground.

"It's Robin," said Emma. "He put two kisses on the Valentine card he sent me."

"What's wrong with that?"

"He knows I hate being double-crossed."

SALLY: Do you really love me?
TOM: Of course I do.
SALLY: Then say something sweet and soft to me.
TOM: Marshmallow, candy floss, Turkish delight . . .

The Egyptian girl was telling her boyfriend how to drive to her house. "And when you get there, don't bother to knock on the door," she said. "Just Toot and Come In!"

EMMA: My boyfriend thinks I've got a face like a million dollars!
THEO: He's right – it's all green and wrinkled!

What did the big candle say to the little candle?
I don't care what you told your boyfriend, you're too young to be going out.

117

My Romantic Fact File

These few pages are rather special because they're all about you – or at least they will be when you've filled them in. By answering the questions you can build up your own romantic fact file and discover who your ideal Valentine is. So reach for your pen and pencil and start answering the questions NOW!

Personal Information
Name: ....
Address: ....
....
Telephone Number: ....
Age: .... Height: ....
Weight: .... Eye colour ....
Hair colour .... Distinguishing marks: ......

Is there a boy or girl you know personally whom you think would make a brilliant Valentine? Yes/No.
If the answer is yes, fill in these questions.
Boy/girl's name: ....
Age: .... Eye colour ....
Hair colour .... Distinguishing marks ......
Rough description: ....

What is it that you particularly like about them? Try to list three things about them that you admire – it could be anything: good looks and a friendly personality or the fact that you both share the same interests.
Three things I admire:
1. ....
2. ....
3. ....

118

Is there anything about them that you're not keen on? Maybe they bite their nails – or perhaps they have an unromantic name like Cyril or Ethel. If there's anything you'd like to change, say so here. The change I'd make: ....

....

Now let's look a little further afield and take into account some other people you might fancy. Which pop star or musician would you most like to make a record with?

....

Which TV star or personality would you most like to appear with?

....

Which movie star would you most like to appear in a film with?

....

Is there anyone else in the public eye – a sports-person, maybe, or perhaps even a politican, who you'd like for a Valentine's Day date?

....

Bearing all the answers you've just given in mind, what would your ideal boyfriend or girlfriend be like? Look back at all the answers you have given to previous questions and see if there are things about each of the people you have named that you'd like your ideal boyfriend or girlfriend to share. Perhaps you'd like your ideal boyfriend to look like Phillip Schofield, dress like Crockett in *Miami Vice*, have Michael J. Fox's sense of humour, and be interested in wildlife like Simon King. Or maybe your perfect girlfriend would look like Kylie Minogue, sing like Madonna, dress like Joan Collins and enjoy sport

like Anneka Rice. (What a very peculiar mixture!)
Now here's *your* chance to choose your ideal
Valentine!

Your Ideal Valentine
How would your ideal Valentine look? Describe
him/her or say who you'd like him/her to look like?

. . . .
. . . .
. . . .

How would you like him/her to dress? Describe the
sort of clothes you'd like him/her to wear.

. . . .
. . . .
. . . .

What sort of personality would he/she have? Would
you like him/her to be noisy and funny, or do you
prefer someone quiet and polite? Is there someone
you know, or someone you've seen whose character
you like?

. . . .
. . . .
. . . .

What special talents would he/she have? Maybe
you'd like to go out with someone who's brilliant at
football or a great dancer? It's your chance to choose!

. . . .
. . . .
. . . .

What kind of things would you have in common?
Most people find that they get along better if they
share the same kind of hobbies, so what would your
ideal Valentine be interested in?

. . . .
. . . .

120